CHAIRING A MEETING
WITH CONFIDENCE

CHAIRING A MEETING WITH CONFIDENCE
An easy guide to rules and procedure

Kevin Paul

Self-Counsel Press
(*a division of*)
International Self-Counsel Press Ltd.
Canada   U.S.A

Printed in Canada

First edition: October, 1989; Reprinted: April, 1990
Second edition: February, 1992

Canadian Cataloguing in Publication Data
Paul, Kevin, 1958-
    Chairing a meeting with confidence
(Self-counsel reference series)
Includes bibliographical references.
ISBN 0-88908-992-2

    1. Meetings.   I. Title.   II. Series.
AS6.P38 1992   658.4'56   C91-091818-X

Self-Counsel Press
(*a division of*)
International Self-Counsel Press Ltd.
Head and Editorial Office
1481 Charlotte Road
North Vancouver, British Columbia V7J 1H1

U.S. Address
1704 N. State Street
Bellingham, Washington 98225

CONTENTS

ACKNOWLEDGMENTS   xi

INTRODUCTION   1

1 BEGINNING THE MEETING   6
   a. Preparation   6
       1. Notice of meeting   6
       2. Agenda   7
       3. Review bylaws and rules of order   9
       4. Anticipation   10
   b. Getting started   10
       1. Call to order and setting the tone   10
       2. Quorum   11
       3. Review agenda   13

2 THE BASICS: DEBATE, MAKING MOTIONS,
   AND VOTING   14
   a. Proceeding in order   14
       1. Routine business   15
       2. Business arising from the previous meeting   17
       3. New business   18
       4. Adjournment   18
   b. Forms of address   19
       1. Addressing the meeting   19
       2. Addressing the chair   19
       3. Addressing other members   20
   c. Making main motions and amendments   20
       1. Making main motions   21

		2.	Debate on main motions	23
		3.	Interrupting debate	24
		4.	Voting on the main motion	25
		5.	Amendments	26
		6.	Amendment to the amendment	28
	d.	Keeping records (minutes)		28
	e.	Ending the meeting		30
		1.	Unfinished business	30
		2.	Review of concluded business	30
		3.	Adjournment	31
		4.	Next meeting	31

3 SOME HELPFUL REMINDERS FOR CHAIRING A SUCCESSFUL MEETING — 32

4 OTHER TYPES OF MOTIONS — 35

			35
a.	Subsidiary motions		35
	1.	Postpone indefinitely	37
	2.	Amend	37
	3.	Commit or refer	37
	4.	Postpone definitely (to a certain time)	38
	5.	Limit or extend debate	39
	6.	Previous question	39
	7.	Lay on the table	41
b.	Privileged motions		42
	1.	Call for the orders of the day	43
	2.	Raise a question of privilege	43
	3.	Take a recess	44
	4.	Adjourn	45
	5.	Fix the time to which to adjourn	45
c.	Incidental motions		46

		1.	Point of order	46
		2.	Appeal the decision of the chair	47
		3.	Suspend the rules	47
	d.	Review of the rankings		48

5 COMMITTEES AND REPORTS 53

	a.	Types of committees		53
		1.	Executive committee	53
		2.	Standing committee	53
		3.	Special or select committee	54
		4.	Committee of the whole	55
	b.	Rules and decorum in committee		55
		1.	The chair	55
		2.	Rules of procedure	56
	c.	Reports of committees		57
		1.	Form of reports	57
		2.	Content of reports	57
		3.	Presentation and consideration of reports	58
		4.	Minority reports	59

6 ELECTIONS 62

	a.	Nominations		62
		1.	By committee	62
		2.	From the floor	63
		3.	Closing nominations	64
	b.	Voting		65
		1.	Counters or tellers	65
		2.	Balloting	65
		3.	Spoiled ballots	66
		4.	Counting the ballots	66
		5.	Announcing the results	67

| | 6. | Plurality or majority | 67 |
| | 7. | Disposal of ballots | 68 |

7   HELP: GOING TO A HIGHER AUTHORITY 69

a.	Parliamentary authority		69
	1.	What is it?	69
	2.	When to use it	70
	3.	Choosing a parliamentary authority	70
	4.	How to include it in your bylaws	71
b.	Professional parliamentarian		72
	1.	What is it?	72
	2.	When to use one	73
	3.	Where to find one	73

8   DO IT YOURSELF: HOW TO WRITE RULES FOR YOUR OWN GROUP 74

a.	Guidelines for developing your own rules		75
	b.	Components of your rules of order	76
	1.	Title	76
	2.	Parliamentary authority	76
	3.	Quorum	76
	4.	Order of business	77
	5.	Length and number of speeches	77
	6.	Methods of voting	78

APPENDIXES

| 1 | Chart of common motions | 79 |
| 2 | Other sources | 81 |

SAMPLES

#1 Meeting agenda   8
#2 Special committee report   60
#3 Permanent committee report   61

TABLES

#1 Summary of the rules of motions   49

ACKNOWLEDGMENTS

I want to thank those people who have directly influenced my interest in parliamentary procedure. Over the years, these friends have either served as my mentors and colleagues in this arcane art or have placed me in positions of trust where I could develop and exercise my skills. I am certain they had no idea what they were fostering, and they are not responsible for any particular opinion or interpretation I have offered in this book. Nonetheless, I owe them a great deal.

If you are very lucky in life, you will meet people whose special qualities give you more than you can possibly repay. While writing this book I was happily aware of the debt I owe Karin Paul, Stephen Howell, Dave Wilson, Duncan Ferguson, and Ruth Wilson.

Most books reach the public bearing only the author's name. But, if the author has been fortunate, the finished product is actually a collaboration. Ruth Wilson and Shannon Edwards edited this book. Their contributions make them my collaborators, and because of their work, the book you are about to use is better than I could have made it by myself.

INTRODUCTION

a. WHO SHOULD USE THIS BOOK?

This book is intended primarily for those people who find themselves in a situation where they have to chair a formal meeting but have little or no experience in the matter. The basic concepts, skills, and information discussed throughout the book are applicable to virtually any type of meeting, from large business meetings conducted at national conventions of associations, to smaller and less formal gatherings of community groups, strata councils, and so on.

This book can also be helpful to the participants in such meetings, even if they are not going to preside. It is always easier and more enjoyable to participate in discussions if you know the rules that will govern them. Many good ideas and suggestions are lost to organizations because members do not know the accepted manner in which to bring their thoughts before the group.

b. HOW TO USE THIS BOOK

This is not a "rule book" on how a meeting should be run. There are many of those kinds of books, and they are not really very helpful if you want a quick introduction to the basics of how to conduct a meeting. In the next three, easy-to-read chapters you will be introduced to the essentials of running a meeting. You will not be inundated with a mass of confusing rules, regulations, procedures, and archaic practices. The latter chapters are meant as supplements to the main "lesson," and should be read only if you wish more detailed preparation or if you are simply interested enough to learn more. A couple of hours of study and practice on your own, using this book as a guide, will prepare you for presiding over, or participating in, just about any type of meeting.

If you have the time and inclination, the study of parliamentary procedure can become a rewarding pastime — even vocation. At the end of this book there is a list of sources for further reading, reference, and participation.

c. WHAT ARE "RULES OF ORDER" AND WHY ARE THEY IMPORTANT?

"Rules of order" and "parliamentary procedure" are general names given to the set of rules, forms, and traditions that have been developed to govern meetings. Taken in their totality, these rules are very confusing and intimidating, and few people can be considered genuine experts in all their intricacies. So why, then, is it necessary to have meetings conducted according to these procedures? If the whole process is so complicated, why bother? The short answer is: BECAUSE THEY WORK. In fact, they work so well that the essence of parliamentary procedure has remained unchanged since its origins in medieval Britain.

The basic purpose of a meeting is to conduct the business of your group in a fair, orderly, and expeditious manner. During the meeting, everyone must feel that they understand what is going on, that they have the chance to voice opinions on the topics discussed, and that the decisions truly reflect the will of the majority of the group. After the meeting, the group must be confident that the business was conducted in a proper manner and that the process used will stand up to any later challenge. The rules of order that have evolved in the western world (particularly in Britain, the Commonwealth, and North America) have proven to be the best way to ensure the satisfactory running of a meeting.

If you belong to an organization that must have formal meetings to make routine as well as important decisions, you know how crucial it is to make those decisions in an organized and coherent manner. Most of us have sat through a really badly run meeting: it is a painful experience and very unsatisfying. The fault of most poorly run meetings lies with the person in the chair.

Chairing a meeting is not difficult. It takes only a little preparation, a little confidence, and a lot of common sense. Add these three factors to the qualities that caused your organization to place you in the chair in the first place, and you have the makings of a good presiding officer. Unfortunately, part of the preparation has often meant plowing through a dense handbook on the rules of order. Without much guidance, practice, or, often, much interest, studying such a book becomes a chore that the newly selected president tries to avoid — and usually does. The result is often loosely run meetings that are an embarrassment to the chair and the group.

What this book will do is prepare you to conduct a meeting of which you and your organization can be proud. If you study the first three short chapters, practice some of the basic forms, and think about your meeting in advance, you should be able to confidently take the chair of your first meeting after only an hour or two of work. You will NOT have to become an expert in *Robert's Rules of Order*, or *Bourinot's Rules of Order*, or any other rule book.

The complete list of rules has become long and complicated because it tries, quite rightly, to cover all the situations that can come up in a meeting. Where people go wrong in their first experiences with parliamentary procedure is in assuming they have to know it all before they can preside over a meeting. We've all run across the obnoxious person at a meeting who insists on strict observance of the letter of the rules, and the chair is not confident enough to stop it. There is also the meeting where no one, including the chair, knows the "official" way to proceed. Both situations are uncomfortable — and unnecessary.

If you know the basics, then, in the vast majority of cases, you know enough to cope with everything likely to arise at your meeting. The rules are more flexible than you may expect: they were devised to serve you and your organization. They are not supposed to get in your way; they are supposed to free you to get on with the efficient running of your group.

d. OFFICIAL RULES OF ORDER

You should not feel bullied into using any so-called "official" book on rules of order. There is no legal requirement that you abide by a particular set of rules. *Robert's Rules of Order* is the most frequently cited authority on parliamentary procedure, and it has become a common misconception that this is the only pattern to follow. It isn't. You and your organization can use any procedure you wish; in fact, you can even create your own. *Robert's* is just one of many books on the subject, and all of them are based on the same essential concepts of how to conduct a meeting. As long as you proceed according to the simple, accepted principles of procedure, you will be on firm ground.

There are many reasons for *Robert's* popularity. It is comprehensive and its format has proven to be very durable. It is, however, more complex than is necessary for most groups. The book you are reading now is all you need to run most meetings. A copy of *Robert's Rules of Order*, or one of its competitors, would not be out of place at your side as something to refer to in extraordinary circumstances, but you should hardly ever need it.

e. HISTORICAL BACKGROUND

The principles and concepts of the rules of order we use today have their origins in the British parliamentary model. They can actually be traced back to the first deliberative assemblies of ancient Greece, but parliamentary procedure with a basis in constitutional behavior and premises began in 13th century England with the Magna Carta. In a form recognizable to us, codified rules of order emerged in the late 18th century and have kept the same relative forms since that time.

The British example has served as a model for most democracies. In Commonwealth countries such as Canada, it has been adopted virtually in its entirety. In the United States, there have been numerous adaptations of British parliamentary procedure, with today's practice tracing a line from Thomas Jefferson through to Henry M. Robert.

In his capacity as vice president and presiding officer in the U.S. Senate, Jefferson used British parliamentary law to write the first set of rules for the Senate. Robert, who was an engineering officer in the United States Army, drew on Jefferson's work for his popular "simplification" of the rules of conducting a meeting. Robert's first book, *Rules of Order*, was published in 1876, and *Robert's Rules of Order Revised* came out in 1915. Both were well received by the public, with the latter becoming an enormous best-seller.

It was this extraordinary early popularity that is most certainly responsible for the dominant position *Robert's* holds in the minds of the public as THE authority on rules of order. There have been many books published on the subject — many as good or better than *Robert's*. Any of these newer works would serve very well as an organization's "parliamentary authority" (see chapter 7 and Appendix 2).

1
BEGINNING THE MEETING

The two vital components to ensuring that you, as the chair of the upcoming meeting, have done all you can to create the possibility of a productive and well-run meeting are —

(a) preparation (well before the meeting begins) and

(b) getting things started properly.

Nothing can substitute for pre-planning and getting things off on the right foot — especially if it is your first meeting. If you do both of these things very well, you will set a tone that will persist throughout the meeting.

a. PREPARATION

Here is a list of activities that anyone presiding at a meeting should do before the event.

(a) Ensure notice of meeting is sent to all members

(b) Prepare an agenda

(c) Review bylaws and rules of order

(d) Anticipate how the meeting will run

Following is a brief discussion of each activity.

1. Notice of meeting

It is usually the responsibility of the secretary of an organization to make certain that all members have been properly notified about the upcoming meeting. This is generally accomplished by a written notice or a phoning committee.

Nevertheless, the president should check that this step is completed properly.

As you take the chair at the meeting, you want to be confident no one can challenge that it is a "properly constituted meeting" of the organization. If your group's bylaws specify how and when meetings are to be called, make certain everything has been done properly. As you gain more experience, you may be able to take this for granted. But at the beginning, your goal is to eliminate all the little sources of worry that can make you nervous at the start of a meeting. Taking care of them personally, or double-checking, does not take much time and can prevent a lot of anxiety.

2. Agenda

An agenda serves two purposes. First, it lists all the routine pieces of business that are often forgotten at the beginning of a meeting. Second, it acts as a program of what will follow after the routine items. A well-designed and detailed agenda can be a great comfort to a nervous chair. Sample #1 gives you an idea of what a good printed agenda should look like.

The items under NEW BUSINESS should be weighted. That is, they should be listed in descending order of importance. If you do this, you will be assured of dealing with the most urgent business first and avoid having to adjourn the meeting without getting to cover necessary items. The catch-all item of OTHER BUSINESS, under the NEW BUSINESS section, gives you the opportunity to let members bring up topics for discussion from the floor, but this is permitted only after the reasons for calling the meeting have been dealt with.

No matter how well you think you know your membership, and no matter how much you try to estimate the time for discussion on each item, it is inevitable that the debate will extend beyond what you planned. Thus, with a weighted agenda, if only one piece of new business gets resolved, it is sure to be the most important.

CALL TO ORDER

ROUTINE BUSINESS

1. Approval of the agenda

2. Approval of the minutes of the previous meeting

3. Communications (read by secretary)

4. Reports

   (a) Chair

   (b) Other officers

   (c) Standing committees

   (d) Special committees

BUSINESS ARISING FROM THE PREVIOUS MEETING

or

UNFINISHED BUSINESS

1. Item under discussion at the adjournment of the last meeting

2. Item prompted by decision or discussion at the last meeting

NEW BUSINESS

1. Most important or most urgent item

2. Second most important or urgent item

3. Third most important or urgent item

4. Other business

ADJOURNMENT

Social Program

Whenever possible, distribute the agenda beforehand, preferably with the notice of meeting. If this is not possible, make sure that the members know a printed agenda will be available at the meeting and encourage them to arrive early so they can examine it.

3. Review bylaws and rules of order

Unless you are an old hand with the details of your organization, it is always a good idea to review your bylaws or constitution before a meeting. There is nothing more embarrassing than to have someone ask how a particular issue corresponds with the bylaws of the organization, and for you, as the president, to be ignorant of its basic rules. Even if you do not know much about the ins and outs of parliamentary law, you must at least know how your own organization is run.

Review the basic rules of order. Most of what you need to know is in chapter 2. Even after you have made a brief study of the rules, always take 10 minutes immediately before the meeting to review the basics. Recite them out loud or write them out on a piece of paper — just to "test" yourself. You should review matters like the following:

- How will I begin the meeting?
- What items have to be voted on?
- How are motions made?
- How does someone make an amendment?
- What are the usual phrases that the chair uses during routine business?
- What are the proper forms of address during the meeting? Is it necessary to stick strictly to formal etiquette?

If you are confident and familiar with the few basic rules and concepts, you will have no difficulty keeping control of the meeting and keeping the respect of the group. Anything more complicated is unlikely to come up at the standard meetings of most organizations. If the unexpected arises, it is perfectly acceptable for the chair to refer to sources and other authorities for assistance (see chapter 7). But to have any credibility as a presiding officer, you must have command of the simple rules of your organization and the essential rules of order.

4. Anticipation

Having spent a few minutes reviewing the general things like bylaws and proper procedure, you will also find it very useful to try to anticipate what is likely to happen at this particular meeting. As the elected/appointed/selected chair of the organization, you are probably in a position to know a great deal about the people you are dealing with, as well as the issues being presented at the upcoming meeting. Are there any members who are likely to cause problems or be disruptive? Are any of the items liable to take a long time to discuss? Are any of the issues particularly contentious?

Try to anticipate any pitfalls that might be created by the people and pieces of business, and prepare answers and strategies for coping in advance. There will always be surprises and things you could not have foreseen, but, with a little advance thinking, you can eliminate most of them. We have all been impressed by the chair who seemed to have anticipated every question, objection, and problem before it was brought up at a meeting. You can project that same aura of competence in your first meeting if you do a little preparation.

b. GETTING STARTED

1. Call to order and setting the tone

Always start the meeting on time. Do not wait for latecomers to arrive. If there are stragglers the first few times you do this, don't worry about it. They will soon discover that the stated time is when the meeting will actually begin. Beginning promptly establishes the authority and business-like approach of the chair. With this relatively minor gesture, members will learn that they can trust you to do what you say, which will make it easier for them to accept your actions on other matters that require decisiveness.

The usual way to begin the meeting (referred to as the Call to Order) is to stand, or strike a gavel once, and state something like "The meeting will now come to order." Do this firmly, confidently, and with authority.

The Call to Order is sometimes the most difficult part of the meeting for an inexperienced chair and one of two things will happen:

(a) all attention will immediately be focused on you, accompanied by a disconcerting sense of expectation — almost as if you are supposed to perform; or

(b) no one will pay much attention to you and the buzz of "pre-meeting gossip" will continue unabated — with the one or two people who heard you expecting you to do something to get everyone else's attention.

It is usually fear of the first that causes the timidity and hesitancy that results in the second. So, perform the Call to Order as firmly as you can. Then, always plan what you will say immediately after you have that focused attention. Quite often this is simply a greeting or welcome:

> *Welcome to the 11th annual meeting of the Maxwell and Marlon Perkins Fan Club. We will now proceed with the routine business.*

2. Quorum

After declaring that the meeting has begun, the first thing that the chair and the secretary must do is to determine if a quorum is present. Quorum is the formal term used to describe the minimum number of members of the organization that must be present in order for that meeting to legally transact business. This minimum number can be a definite number or a proportion of the existing membership (e.g., 25 members or 25% of the membership).

The requirement for quorum should be defined in the constitution or bylaws of the organization. If it is not defined, the conventions of parliamentary law prescribe that a quorum is a majority of the membership. For most groups this is not realistic and that is why a lower number is usually set. When determining or reviewing what a quorum should be for your organization, common sense should prevail. A general rule for quorum is that it need not be any larger than the number of people normally expected to attend any meeting.

The reason for setting a quorum is to protect the organization from having decisions made by a small group — unless such a group is specifically given that authority (e.g., an executive committee).

If a quorum is not present at the outset of a meeting, the presiding officer announces this fact, and the meeting should be adjourned immediately. This is usually a temporary adjournment to allow time for latecomers to make up the quorum. Convening the meeting and then adjourning is preferable to simply waiting for others to arrive because it places the onus on members to be on time.

Whenever the situation of a lack of quorum arises, the chair should explain it to the members present. Except for some "housekeeping" motions that are dealt with in more detailed books, any decisions made in the absence of a quorum are not valid and the members of the organization are not bound by them. So, as the chair, you must not let yourself be convinced by others that the meeting should proceed in the absence of a quorum in the hope that a quorum will be met later in the meeting, or that the decisions of this "illegal" meeting will not be challenged. It is rarely in the best interests of the organization to conduct meetings without a quorum; if the issues for discussion are important enough to warrant calling a meeting, then they are important enough to be dealt with by a properly constituted meeting.

3. Review agenda

Before the first item of routine business, it is often a good idea to review the agenda for the membership. This is especially important if there are new or inexperienced members present. Let them know how the meeting will proceed and what will happen at each stage. If you are a novice chair, this step can be yet another way to ease into the meeting. It also assists in the goals of establishing a tone of authority and concern for the understanding and participation of all members. Remember, a good meeting should end with all the members feeling that they knew what went on and that they were given a chance to have their say.

2
THE BASICS: DEBATE, MAKING MOTIONS, AND VOTING

There would be no need for rules of order if there were an unlimited amount of time to discuss issues and if human beings could be depended on to always be courteous, succinct, and logical. Since neither ideal is likely to be evident at all times in human activities, the principles of parliamentary procedure are a great help in engendering such qualities — at least during meetings. Rules of order provide a framework within which meaningful discussion and decision making can take place. The rules recognize that time is often in short supply and that people, especially in the midst of heated debate, will not always be on their best behavior.

The traditions for proceeding with the discussion and resolution of issues are important. To many people these traditions may seem far too formal and persnickety. The formality is a necessary mechanism for ensuring the principle of fairness to both the majority and the minority. If the precision of the process seems to be getting in the way, it is usually because the person in the chair is not exercising sufficient control or providing enough guidance and explanation to the membership.

a. PROCEEDING IN ORDER

The first and most obvious form of this formality is having the meeting proceed according to the order set down in the agenda. This is the first substantive opportunity for the chair to begin to exert an influence over the meeting. You must make certain that everyone at the meeting is clear about

14

which item is currently under discussion, what action must be taken (if any), and when that item has been disposed of.

1. Routine business

The items listed under routine business on the agenda (approval of the agenda, approval of the minutes of previous meetings, communications and reports) can often be dealt with very quickly. The degree of formality you use to move through this part of the agenda can vary a great deal and will depend on the circumstances of the meeting. At a large and important meeting, it may be appropriate to ask for motions and votes on all things. At smaller, more regular meetings, the chair can often assume consent for these basic items unless someone actually raises a point or an objection. It is up to you to exercise your best judgment in this matter. If you are unsure, it is best to opt for the more formal approach. Later, as you gain more confidence and experience, you can alter your style.

(a) Approval of the agenda

Approval of the agenda is an optional step that, if included, should be the first piece of routine business. It is more than the simple review of the agenda discussed in the previous chapter. Quite often this is a formality that can be dispensed with. There may, however, be times when the composition of the agenda itself is a contentious issue, especially if there is more business than can usually be dealt with at a single meeting. If this item appears on the agenda, it gives the membership an opportunity to make changes. If no changes are suggested or approved, then a formal vote ensures that acceptance of the agenda will appear in the record of the meeting.

When all discussion is finished, the chair usually asks for a motion for approval:

May I have a motion to approve the agenda?

15

This motion requires a seconder and must be approved by a majority vote.

(b) Approval of the minutes of the previous meeting

The minutes of the previous meeting should be circulated beforehand. If they have not been, you should allow some time for the members to review them. The form for approving the minutes is the same as for the agenda. After any discussion and corrections, the chair asks for a motion:

May I have a motion to approve the minutes of the last meeting?

This motion also requires a seconder and must be approved by a majority vote.

Approving the minutes provides proof in the records of your organization that the minutes of each meeting were reviewed and are an accurate representation of what occurred at any particular meeting. The amount of detail in the minutes of your organization will determine how much time this item takes up. If only votes are recorded, then the record will be sparse and not likely to create much discussion. If verbatim or paraphrased reports of debate are kept, then there may be differences of opinion about their accuracy.

Regardless of the level of detail in your minutes, the purpose of discussion on this point is to ensure accuracy. You must be very careful not to allow a re-opening of the actual issue that was discussed.

(c) Communications

Communications are usually letters addressed to the organization or its officers. In the routine business part of the meeting, communications are read for the information of the members. They are read at this stage of the meeting so it will appear in the record that they were received and heard by the members present. If there is any action to be taken from the communication, that will appear as an item under "New Business."

(d) Reports

As executive members of your organization, the various officeholders (president, treasurer, etc.) are responsible to the entire group and should report on their activities. This is an informational function, much like the reading of communications, which is why it appears as routine business.

This is also the appropriate time to hear from any committees. It may be that your organization requires certain committees to report at every meeting. Some committees may have an interim or final report to offer. Again, this is for information only. In all cases, if there is action required or suggested by a report, it should become an item of business.

The usual motion at this stage is to accept the report of the officer or committee. This can be done by the chair simply declaring acceptance in the absence of any objection. The chair will use a declaration such as —

> *If there are no objections, the minutes will record that the report is received with thanks.*

Acceptance does not necessarily imply members' approval; it simply acknowledges receipt. While debate on specific issues raised in the report is out of order in this part of the meeting, it is possible to discuss the work of the committee in general (i.e., a motion to censure a committee that has failed to report for several meetings).

2. Business arising from the previous meeting

There are two types of issues that should be dealt with before proceeding to any new business:

(a) Any matter that was under discussion at the end of the previous meeting but was not resolved

(b) Any matter that clearly must be dealt with as a result of what occurred at the previous meeting

Specific rules govern how to handle ending a meeting when you are in the middle of a discussion. This situation is explained in greater detail later in this chapter (see section **e. ENDING THE MEETING** on page 30).

3. New business

As was mentioned in chapter 1, the list of items under this heading should be weighted. That is, the most important or urgent items should be first, and the rest listed in descending order of importance. Importance and urgency are, of course, subjective concepts, and, therefore, there are liable to be differences of opinion about the order. Any controversy of this sort must be disposed of during the approval of the agenda portion of routine proceedings. After that there should be no further discussion about the order of the agenda. As the chair, it is up to you to quell any such debate. Concern about the shortage of time is most likely to occur as the end of the meeting becomes imminent.

4. Adjournment

There are specific rules dealing with adjournment. (See section **e. ENDING THE MEETING** on page 30). This stage can often be confusing for the less experienced members, so you should be clear on the rules of adjournment and be ready to explain "what happens now."

Once the meeting is officially adjourned, there is no more debate. Any continuing discussion is unofficial and off the record. Once the meeting is officially adjourned, you are no longer in the chair and you should not entertain motions or conduct any official business or action. This may seem painfully obvious, but the impulse to continue talking after the majority has already made a decision is very strong in some people — especially if the debate has been a heated one. The

18

chair must be firm in enforcing adjournment once it has been approved.

b. FORMS OF ADDRESS

Another aspect of formality that is important to the proper conduct of a business meeting is how you address the people at that meeting. This is known as observing proper decorum. As with other facets of parliamentary procedure, this is also a rather flexible concept: the degree of formality in the forms of address is, quite rightly, variable among organizations and among the different kinds of meetings within the same organizations. The weekly meeting of a strata council of six or seven people will be much less formal than the annual general meeting of a corporation or a national association attended by several hundred.

1. Addressing the meeting

Before anyone may address the meeting, he or she must be recognized by the chair. The basic rule of keeping order in any meeting is that only one person should speak at one time. It is the prerogative of the chair to decide who is to speak. The chair usually does this by indicating the person who is to speak next. In a very formal meeting, the usual form is to say

The chair recognizes _____.

Once recognized, that person then "has the floor" until his or her remarks are either concluded or are interrupted by a procedural objection from the membership or the chair (see section **c. 3. Interrupting debate** on page 24).

2. Addressing the chair

Just what may be the proper form of address to the person in the chair has become a matter of some controversy in recent years. For hundreds of years, the acceptable term was chairman, regardless of whether the presiding officer was a man or a woman. Recently, however, this term has come to be

19

regarded by some as a sexist epithet. There has been a continuing, if rather unsatisfactory, search for alternatives such as chairwoman or chairperson.

Throughout this book the neutral word "chair" has been employed. Some people become upset with having to abandon traditional usage, while others object strenuously to that tradition. Consequently, many people at a meeting now have the added burden of being unsure which title or form of address is likely to cause offense.

If the organization has made no definitive statement in its own rules or bylaws, the best guideline to follow is to allow the person in the chair to be called whatever he or she deems appropriate. If the preference is for chairman, or chairwoman, or chairperson, the members present are bound to respect that. It is incumbent on the chair to inform the meeting of that preference as soon as possible.

3. Addressing other members

Simple courtesy should guide you when addressing other members. In small assemblies, that is all that need be said. In larger meetings, it is appropriate to follow the parliamentary custom of all remarks being addressed to, or "through," the chair even if intended for the audience in general or one member in particular. An example of this kind of address is the following:

> *Mr. Chairman, I would like to respond to the statement of my esteemed colleague.*

The remarks are obviously meant for everyone at the meeting, but are addressed to the meeting through the chair.

c. MAKING MAIN MOTIONS AND AMENDMENTS

Aside from those matters automatically brought up by virtue of their being routine proceedings or unfinished business or business arising from the previous meeting, matters come before the meeting through the process of making motions.

There are many types of motions possible in the course of a meeting. Some are merely "housekeeping" or procedure motions, and some are substantive or main motions. Main motions are the way in which most of the business of your organization is accomplished. A motion is basically a proposal that the organization take a certain action on a matter or that it officially adopt a certain policy on an issue. Once a subject has been brought before the meeting through a motion, it can be discussed and a decision, if one is necessary, can be made. Since main motions are frequently framed imperfectly, or give rise to differences of opinion, there is a mechanism, known as amendment, for adjusting them.

The various classes and types of motions have a rank according to their precedence in debate. When a motion of a particular rank has been made, some other ranks are "out of order." The differences between these motions can be very confusing, and it is not something novices need be concerned with during their first meetings.

A good chair should eventually learn all the types of motions and their ranks, but, for the purpose of this book, the proper order of motions is explained in general terms. (A table of the rankings is supplied in Appendix 1.)

Knowing how to deal with main motions and their accompanying amendments is one of the most basic skills of chairing a meeting, and that is the subject of most of this chapter. Other types of motions are described in chapter 4.

1. Making main motions

A member of the organization may make a motion if he or she gains the floor — having been recognized by the chair — and the motion is in order. A main motion is considered in order if there is no other business before the meeting and it is pertinent to the next or current item on the agenda. (There

21

are some special motions that are always in order; see chapter 4.) It is up to the chair to determine if a motion is in order.

To be valid, a main motion must be seconded by another member. There is a good reason for this step. It is a way of ensuring that at least two members of the group wish the motion to be debated. This requirement avoids one particular member wasting the time of the meeting with frivolous discussion. If there is no one willing to second a motion, it "dies" and the floor of the meeting is again open. Seconding a motion does not necessarily mean that the seconder agrees with the motion — only that it should be discussed.

Once a motion has been moved and seconded and is deemed to be in order, the chair should restate the exact motion so that the entire meeting is clear about what is to be discussed. At this point the matter is open for discussion.

A typical example of this sequence is as follows:

Chair: *We will now go on to item #2 under New Business, which deals with the matter of a new constitution for our association.*

Member #1: *Madam Chair.*

Chair: *The chair recognizes Mr. X.*

Member #1: *Thank you, Madam Chair. I move that we form a committee to deal with drafting a new constitution and that the committee consist of four people elected by this meeting.*

Chair: *Is there a seconder for this motion?*

Member #2: *Yes, Madam Chair, I will second that.*

Chair: *It has been moved by Mr. X., seconded by Ms. Z, that "We form a committee to deal with drafting a new constitution and that the committee consist of four people elected by this meeting." The floor is now open for discussion.*

This is more formal than you may require for your particular meeting, but the essential process and intent remains the same regardless of the style of speech employed.

2. Debate on main motions

Once the question is formally before the meeting by having been moved and seconded, the custom is for the mover of the motion to speak first. This privilege is not universal, nor is it required that the mover speak at all. In most cases, this precedence is given so that the mover may introduce the rationale for the motion and provide basic information. It is common for smaller, informal assemblies to allow members to question the mover during this first speech.

In addition to the principles of decorum and courtesy that should be observed in all debate, the concept of relevance is something to which you must pay particular attention. After a duly moved and seconded motion is before the meeting, all discussion must deal specifically with the subject of that motion. When the remarks of any particular member begin to stray from the topic at hand, it is the duty of the chair to interrupt the speaker and insist that debate be to the point.

During debate it is the responsibility of the chair to act as a neutral voice. This certainly does not mean that the chair is not permitted to have opinions on the matter under consideration. It does mean, however, that he or she must refrain from expressing those opinions. the authority of the chair depends on the meeting's confidence that he or she will be an impartial facilitator. If bias on one side of the question becomes obvious, you will have undermined one of the main objectives of any meeting — that of ensuring that the process was fair. While you are in the chair, you only job is to guide the meeting.

However, since the chair is a valued member of the group, each organization should have a mechanism that will allow that person to engage in debate. The most effective way to accomplish this is to make sure one of the officers is designated as vice chair (usually a vice president or other senior member). When the person presiding over the meeting wishes to participate in the debate, the usual form is to inform the meeting that he or she is relinquishing the chair for that purpose. The designated person then assumes the chair.

When the chair steps down to take part in debate, it is not possible to resume the chair until that particular motion has been put to a vote. If the designated vice chair has already spoken on the issue, then the chair may select another qualified individual to preside temporarily. Once the question on which the original chair expressed an opinion has been decided, that person resumes the chair.

3. Interrupting debate

Once a member "has the floor," he or she should not be interrupted. It is the duty of the chair to ensure that this privilege is observed. However, there are times when it is acceptable to interrupt a member who is speaking.

If, during the course of his or her remarks, the member violates any rules of order, the chair or any other member may intrude on the debate. The chair's interruption usually takes the following form:

Order please, the member is out of order.

At this point, the member must stop speaking while the chair explains the violation. Typical offenses are irrelevance, excessive repetition, offensive language, and making an improper motion.

Another member may bring the infraction to the attention of the chair by declaring —

Point of order, Madam Chair.

In this case, the chair asks the offending member to cease talking while the alleged breach of the rules of order is

24

explained. (See chapter 4 for an explanation of a point of order.) After the violation and remedy have been explained to the speaker, it is customary to allow his or her speech to continue. Repeated infringement is usually punished by loss of the floor.

The chair must deal with interruptions of points of order as quickly and firmly as possible. The goal is to enforce the rules, but not allow them to impede discussion.

4. Voting on the main motion

Once debate has clearly been exhausted, the chair puts the issue that has been discussed to a vote. This is commonly referred to as "putting the question." If members of the meeting wish the vote to take place, they are said to "call the question." The *question* is whether or not the motion on the floor should pass.

Part of protecting the rights of the minority and the individual means making certain that everyone has had the opportunity to speak on an issue. Therefore, even if the discussion has gone on for a long time, and the majority of members are becoming restive, it is the chair's responsibility to permit anyone to speak who still wishes to do so. The chair should resist calls from the audience to "put the question" and "let's get on with it." (There is a special motion that can be used to force a vote even if there are others who wish to speak; see chapter 4.)

The motion, either in its original form or as amended, if it has been altered (see below), is read by the presiding officer:

> *There being no further debate, I will recognize the call for the question. It has been moved by Mr. X, seconded by Ms. Z, that "We form a committee to deal with drafting a new constitution and that the committee consist of four people elected by this meeting."*

Those in favor of the motion are asked to signal their assent by raising their hands or saying "Aye." Those opposed are then asked to raise their hands or say "Nay." The chair then announces whether the motion is carried or defeated.

For most motions, the method of voting depends on the custom of your organization or the preference of the chair. There are times when it is better to conduct a secret ballot than to record the show of hands (e.g., when officers are being elected). Generally, however, it is enough for the chair to interpret the strength of the voice vote or show of hands. If any member disputes the result as announced, the chair should ask for a recorded vote to make certain of the decision. In order to pass, a main motion requires the affirmative vote of a simple majority of those present (i.e., at least 50% plus one).

5. Amendments

Once a main motion is before the meeting, it can be amended. Members are free to offer as many changes as they like until the main motion accurately reflects the will of the majority.

To present an amendment, a member must first obtain the floor in the usual way. Another speaker cannot be interrupted. Although there is no obligation to do so, an experienced presiding officer will frequently give preference to recognizing someone who obviously wishes to make an amendment.

An amendment must be moved and seconded just like a main motion. Whenever possible, the amendment should be in written form. This is for the benefit of the recording secretary and the chair; the amendment process can become very confusing and anything that helps to keep track of all proposals is worth doing.

The chair must insist that all amendments be specifically worded. It is useless for someone to move an amendment that simply says "I move that we change the number of people on the constitution committee."

As an example, a properly worded amendment looks like this:

Member #3:   *Madam Chair, I move that the number "four" be deleted, and the number "seven" substituted for it.*

If the main motion had contained more than one reference to the number four, then the proposed amendment must be even more specific:

Member #3:   *Madam Chair, I move that the number "four" between the words "of" and "people" be deleted, and the number "seven" substituted for it.*

The chair should re-state the motion for amendment, just as with a main motion. A good presiding officer will also read how the main motion would change if the amendment is passed:

> *It has been moved by Member #3, seconded by Member #4, that the motion be amended by the deletion of the number "four" between the words "of" and "people" and the number "seven" substituted for it. If this amendment is carried, the main motion would then be that "We form a committee to deal with drafting a new constitution and that this committee consist of seven people elected by this meeting."*

Now the subject for debate can only be about whether or not the committee should consist of four or seven people. The chair must pay close attention to the relevance of members' remarks.

If an amendment is defeated, the original main motion is automatically before the meeting again. If an amendment is passed, the main motion automatically comes before the meeting **in its changed form.** Debate continues as before — either on the main motion or on another amendment.

The chair should make it clear to everyone what has happened when a vote is taken on an amendment. For example:

> *The amendment has been defeated. Therefore, we have now resumed consideration of the original motion. The debate must be directed to the main motion, or you may introduce new amendments.*
>
> -or-
>
> *The amendment passes. Therefore, we are now considering the original motion IN ITS AMENDED FORM. [Restate amended motion.]*

6. Amendment to the amendment

Traditional rules of procedure allow members to make motions that amend an amendment already on the floor. Inexperienced chairs should avoid this kind of motion as it is not really necessary. In the vast majority of situations, it is rare to have an amendment so complex that an amendment to the amendment is appropriate. In nearly all situations, such motions can be dealt with as separate amendments.

The best strategy is to tell the meeting that the chair will entertain only one amendment at a time — that is, there will be no amendments to amendments. This will do a great deal to save the sanity of the chair and the membership.

d. KEEPING RECORDS (MINUTES)

There should always be a written record kept of all formal business meetings of your organization. Such an account is usually called the minutes of the meeting and is the responsibility of the secretary of the organization. It is also common practice for the chair to oversee the correct recording of proceedings and to work with the secretary to ensure its accuracy.

The format of the record keeping and the level of detail recorded depends on the custom and needs of the organization. At the very least, your group's minutes should contain the following information:

(a) Kind of meeting (i.e., regular, special or extraordinary, or adjourned)

(b) Name of the organization

(c) The time, date, and place of the meeting

(d) The name of the secretary and the presiding officer

(e) The names of those present and absent if the meeting is of an executive or other committee (This is unnecessary, if not impossible, for much larger gatherings.)

(f) Routine business — especially the approval of the previous minutes and any corrections noted

(g) The movers and seconders (optional) of all main motions and the results of the votes on all main motions as amended (It is not necessary to record the original motion or the amendments.)

(h) The time of adjournment

The final copies should bear the signatures of both the secretary and the presiding officer.

If more expansive minutes are desired, other matters that may appropriately be recorded are the following:

(a) Points of order raised, as well as any appeals made (The ruling of the chair should also be included.)

(b) Any other motions that are carried

(c) The main ideas or arguments presented during debate on a main motion (It is not necessary to record discussions word for word.)

For more information on taking effective minutes, see *The Minute Taker's Handbook*, another title in the Self-Counsel Series.

e. ENDING THE MEETING

The manner in which a meeting ends is just as important as how it begins. The chair must make certain that the goals of fairness and comprehension have been achieved, and the members must feel that the meeting has been conducted with propriety and that they have understood everything.

When the time comes to stop the meeting, there are a number of things that have to be dealt with by the chair.

1. Unfinished business

If the meeting must end at an appointed time (see section 3. **Adjournment** below), it is quite likely that the hour will arrive in the midst of discussion of an agenda item. When this occurs, the chair must be firm in ending the meeting as required. However, the chair should also make it clear to the membership how and when consideration of the issue will be renewed:

> *The meeting is now over. Debate on this question will be renewed as the first item under "Unfinished Business" on the agenda of the next regular meeting.*

2. Review of concluded business

A good presiding officer will always try to recap the main decisions made during a meeting. This is especially helpful if it has been a long, complex meeting and if any of the decisions have resulted in work being assigned to any members. It can be yet another way in which you attempt to make everyone feel that they have understood what went on at the meeting. A small action like this at the end of a meeting can go a long way toward maintaining group harmony.

3. Adjournment

Always announce that the meeting is adjourned. Do not allow things to simply disintegrate after the last piece of business. Finish with the same exhibition of control with which you began.

Formal adjournment usually requires an actual motion with a seconder. Most often, however, adjournment is announced by the chair asking if there is any further business. If there is none, the chair can say "If there is no further business, and no objection, the meeting is adjourned." The members agree to this by silent consent.

Adjournment is ALWAYS in the control of the members. The process of silent consent gives the appearance that it is the prerogative of the chair, but that is not the case.

There is further discussion of adjournment and the various motions concerning it in chapter 4 (see section **b. PRIVILEGED MOTIONS**).

4. Next meeting

Whenever possible and appropriate, conclude the meeting by announcing the time and place of the next meeting.

3
SOME HELPFUL REMINDERS FOR CHAIRING A SUCCESSFUL MEETING

Presented here is a summary of helpful hints for chairing a meeting. They should be used as a review and not as a replacement for study of the previous two chapters.

- Always prepare before the meeting. This does not have to mean doing a great deal of homework and practice, but neither should it be ignored altogether.

- If you are unsure about the correct phrases and forms of speech, review chapters 1 and 2 and pay particular attention to the samples of motions, etc.

- Start the meeting on time. Do not wait for stragglers.

- Adopt the attitude that you are there to assist the meeting, NOT to run or control it. You preside at the pleasure of the assembly and you are its servant. Remember that your duty is to enforce the rules of the organization, not your own!

- Review procedure or process when it seems to be getting involved or confusing.

- Before allowing any debate, always read all motions out loud to the meeting as soon as they are properly moved. Do so again just before they are voted on.

- During debate, keep track of those trying to get your attention and try to be fair in your recognition of speakers. In a large group it is a good idea to keep a list of members waiting their turn to speak and those who have already spoken.

- During debate, PAY ATTENTION TO THE SPEAK-ERS. Do not let your attention wander. This is more than just a matter of courtesy; you never know when you will have to rule on something the speaker has said. Pay particular attention to relevance.

- When ruling on points of order, deciding the next order of business, announcing the results of votes, etc., be firm and clear. This does not mean you should appear as an autocrat and take great pleasure in overruling others. Do not become enamored of your "power."

- If a procedural matter arises and you are not sure how to resolve it, NEVER TRY TO BLUFF! There is no shame in not having the answer at your fingertips. The best thing to do is call a brief recess and consult a bona fide rule book. Remember, your primary concern should be to get it right. If you have mastered the basics in this book, such a situation should rarely arise and you will be ready for most things. But, if it does, you will probably have the respect of the members and they will appreciate your deliberation much more than a snow job!

- Make sure you know the constitution and bylaws of your organization.

- Provide leadership for the meeting. Make an effort to keep order and maintain appropriate decorum. There is a fine line between being "on a power trip" and keeping order as a function of enforcing the rights of the members to a well run and orderly meeting. Be aware of that line, but do not shy away from enforcing order. The rest of the members are depending on you. Another aspect of leadership is offering advice. Remaining impartial on the particular issue at hand does not preclude the chair from offering suggestions to members on such matters as how to frame their motions or what the consequences of a particular action might be.

- Remain impartial and do not engage in debate.
- Pay particular attention to time. The length of time that an individual member has spoken, the amount of time spent on a particular item of business, and the approaching time of adjournment are all factors of which a good chair should be constantly aware.

4

OTHER TYPES OF MOTIONS

With the exception of motions to amend, adjourn, and raise a point of order, the motions discussed in this chapter will not occur very often in a normal meeting. However, they are introduced here to make you aware of their existence and what they mean. A brief description only is provided here; if you ever need a more detailed explanation, you should refer to one of the more comprehensive books on rules of order.

When working in the realm of different classes of motions other than a main motion, the chair is faced with a myriad of nuances and peculiarities about the correct procedure to follow in each case. There are five important questions to consider with each of the motions discussed below:

(a) Can such a motion interrupt another speaker?

(b) Does the motion require a seconder?

(c) Is the motion debatable?

(d) Can this motion be amended?

(e) What is required for the motion to pass (i.e., a simple majority vote, a two-thirds majority, no vote at all)?

It is not necessary, at this point, for you to memorize all the permutations of these details. Table #1 at the end of this chapter provides a summary of these factors. In addition, a chart has been provided in Appendix 1 for your reference.

a. SUBSIDIARY MOTIONS

Subsidiary motions are a specific class of motion that may be made while a main motion is under consideration. They provide different ways of dealing with a main motion besides simply debating it and voting on it.

As the term subsidiary implies, there must be a main motion on the floor before any of these motions are in order. All subsidiary motions require a seconder. There are seven subsidiary motions and they have a definite rank among them. They are discussed in more detail in the following sections. Here they are listed from lowest to highest rank.

(1) Postpone indefinitely

(2) Amend

(3) Commit or refer

(4) Postpone definitely (to a certain time)

(5) Limit or extend debate

(6) Previous question

(7) Lay on the table

To avoid confusion about which motion is in order at which time, this concept of rank has evolved. It may seem complex, but is actually quite simple once explained. The basic principle is that when a particular subsidiary motion is pending, all motions of higher rank are in order, and all those ranking lower are out of order.

For example, if there is an amendment to a main motion, then a motion to postpone to a definite time would be in order because it ranks higher than a motion to amend. But a motion to postpone indefinitely would be out of order because it has a lower rank than an amendment.

If there is an amendment to a main motion, a motion to lay on the table would be in order. Because that motion has the highest rank, none of the other six can be moved or debated until the motion to lay on the table has been properly decided.

For example, if the meeting has before it a motion to limit debate, and someone tries to move that the matter be "postponed indefinitely," the chair should respond:

> *That motion is out of order. Because it is a lower ranking subsidiary motion than the one already on the floor, it cannot be considered at this time.*

1. Postpone indefinitely

This is an odd motion because it does not genuinely postpone the main motion. The only purpose and effect of the motion to postpone indefinitely is to kill the main motion without actually voting against it.

2. Amend

The motion to amend is the most widely used subsidiary motion and is discussed in detail in chapter 2. To make your life easier, it is worth repeating that you should avoid the use of the amendment to an amendment motion; allow only one amendment at a time. Remember that amendments must be specific and relevant to the main motion.

3. Commit or refer

The purpose of a motion to commit or refer is to send the main motion to a committee. It is proposed when the main motion requires more discussion or in-depth investigation than is possible by the meeting of the entire membership. The issue of how committees are set up, and how they should act and report, can get very complex. Some of these matters are dealt with in chapter 5. However, much of the possible confusion can be alleviated if the initial motion to commit or refer is specific and well thought out. To this end, the motion to commit or refer should include the following information:

(a) Size of the committee

(b) Method of selecting the committee members

(c) Terms of reference (i.e., exactly what the committee is expected to deal with)

(d) When the committee must report back to the main assembly

An example of a properly worded motion to commit or refer is the following:

> *I move that the main motion, along with pending amendments, be referred to a committee of five people to be selected by the executive. The committee will investigate the matter and report its recommendations at the next quarterly meeting.*

All of the four limiting factors are potentially contentious, so a motion to commit or refer is amendable.

4. Postpone definitely (to a certain time)

This motion refers to the main motion and puts off discussion of the motion before the meeting until a specific time. That specific time is either at the next meeting of the organization or later in the same meeting. Examples of the proper form of such motions are as follows:

> *Madam President, I move that consideration of this matter be postponed until 3:15 p.m.*

> *Mr. Chairman, I move that consideration of this matter be postponed until Resolution #2 has been dealt with.*

> *Madam Chair, I move that this motion be postponed until the next regular meeting.*

It is the duty of the chair to make sure that the postponed item comes before the meeting at the stipulated time. If the decision is to postpone to the next meeting, the chair must place the item on the agenda as unfinished business.

5. Limit or extend debate

A motion to limit or extend debate is important, although it is rarely necessary in small groups or at routine meetings. It deals with the power of the membership to impose limits on debate or to eliminate some limits that already exist. There are several situations that can be affected by such motions:

- To limit total time for debate on a motion
- To limit the number of times any member may speak on a motion
- To limit the time for any individual speech
- To set the time for closing debate and voting on the motion
- To extend the time that a member may speak
- To extend the time for debate past the usual adjournment time

Following are some examples of this type of motion:

I move that members be allowed only one speech of five minutes.

I move that discussion on this motion be limited to not more that 20 minutes.

I move that the current speaker's time be extended by 10 minutes.

6. Previous question

This is perhaps the most ill-named motion in the canon of parliamentary procedure. Its object is to immediately close debate and bring the question to a vote. This motion is not amendable or debatable and is especially useful for ending debate quickly if time is being squandered on repetitious or frivolous debate.

Because adoption of this motion shuts off debate and may deprive some members of their right to speak, parliamentary law dictates that passage requires a two-thirds majority.

The two common forms of such a motion are —

I move the previous question.

-or-

I move that the question be now put.

If passed, the motion under debate at the time is IMMEDIATELY voted on. There is no further debate of any sort allowed once the previous question has been carried.

If it is phrased in the manner described above, the motion for the previous question refers only to matter immediately under discussion. If there are other motions on the floor (e.g., a main motion and an amendment), they are not affected by adoption of the previous question. For example, if there is a main motion, then an amendment, then a motion to refer to a committee, and then someone moves a simple version of the previous question, it deals only with the motion to refer to a committee. If something more comprehensive is desired, then the motion for the previous question must clearly reflect that. In this case you might say the following:

I move the previous question on all pending motions.

-or-

I move that the question be now put on the main motion and all pending subsidiary motions.

If a comprehensive version is carried, then the chair must begin to put all pending motions to a vote without any further debate on any of them — commencing with the highest ranking subsidiary motion (if any) and concluding with the main motion.

If the motion is passed, the chair should say —

> *The motion to put the question has been carried. We must, therefore, move immediately to a vote on the motion currently on the floor.*

The chair then conducts a vote in the usual manner. No further debate is allowed. If the "previous question" motion is defeated, the chair should say —

> *The motion to put the question has been defeated. Debate will now resume on the motion currently on the floor.*

7. Lay on the table

This is the highest ranking of subsidiary motions. Its effect is to temporarily set aside a main motion and any subsidiary motions concerned with the main motion. The proper forms of the motion are the following:

> *I move to lay the main motion, and its associated subsidiary motions, on the table.*

> *I move that the main motion and all subsidiary motions be tabled.*

The motion to lay on the table differs from that to postpone indefinitely because there is a mechanism to recover an item from the table, while postponing indefinitely banishes the issue forever. The primary use of this kind of motion is to allow the meeting to move on to another piece of business even though the current matter is not resolved. This usually happens when it appears likely that a particular debate will take too long for the time allotted and there is other important business.

The motion to lay on the table also differs from that to postpone definitely (to a certain time) because postponing definitely becomes the responsibility of the chair while it is postponed, and a motion can only be lifted from the table by a motion from the membership (see section **c. INCIDENTAL MOTIONS** below).

b. PRIVILEGED MOTIONS

Privileged motions rank above both subsidiary motions and main motions. As their general name implies, they hold a privileged place in the order of business during a meeting. They never relate directly to any pending question, but are given precedence because they deal with issues requiring immediate attention.

Like subsidiary motions, privileged motions have a defined rank among themselves. Because of this high rank, privileged motions are not debatable: they must be decided immediately. (Please check the motion chart in Appendix 1 for details about whether these motions can interrupt a speaker, need a seconder, etc.) There are some peculiarities in this class of motion that are best explained by a detailed book on rules of order.

The privileged motions are listed below from lowest to highest rank.

(1) Call for the orders of the day

(2) Raise a question of privilege

(3) Take a recess

(4) Adjourn

(5) Fix the time to which to adjourn

The principle of ranking that affects subsidiary motions also operates with privileged motions. When a particular motion is on the floor, those of higher rank are in order, and those of lower rank are out of order.

1. Call for the orders of the day

This is a motion used when the chair is deviating from the orders of the day (i.e., the agenda) or when another member introduces a topic that is not the next prescribed order of business. A call for the order of the day is a method for the membership to get a meeting back on track. Any member can make this motion and it is not necessary for the mover to receive the recognition of the chair. The form is simply —

Madam Chair, I call for the orders of the day.

This motion is not debatable and requires a two-thirds negative response to be defeated. The chair must put it to an immediate vote with the following statement:

The orders of the day have been called for. Those who are in favor of proceeding with the orders of the day will say AYE. Those opposed will say NAY.

Since the vote is less than two-thirds in the negative, the motion is carried. We will proceed immediately to the next order of business.

2. Raise a question of privilege

A question of privilege is a matter relating to the comfort, safety, rights, reputation, etc. of the assembly as a whole or any individual member. It can be raised at any time, even to interrupt a speaker. Questions of privilege are usually quite simple things, but certainly no less important for their simplicity. The object is to obtain immediate action on matters such as heating, lighting, audibility of speakers, etc.

The chair must immediately decide whether the matter is, in fact, a valid question of privilege, and then take appropriate action. There is no voting unless the chair's decision is appealed.

Here is a sample sequence for raising and dealing with a question of privilege:

Member: *Madam President, I rise on a question of privilege affecting the assembly.*

            -or-

            Madam President, I rise on a question of personal privilege.

Chair: *The member will state his question of privilege.*

Member: *Those of us in the back rows cannot hear the speakers at the front. Would it be possible to close the doors so the noise from the hall does not interfere?*

Chair: *If there is no objection, your request is granted.* (Wait for objections.) *You may close the doors.*

3. Take a recess

A recess is a short intermission in the proceedings. If the agenda does not specifically allow for a recess, then it can only occur as the result of passing the appropriate motion. If a motion to recess is made when another motion is pending, it is a privileged motion. If it is made when no other business is under consideration, it is treated as a main motion. The motion to recess must be specific about time, and that aspect of it can be amended:

> *Madam President, I move that we recess for 10 minutes.*

> -or-

> *Mr. Chair, I move that the meeting recess until 7:15 p.m.*

If carried, the recess occurs immediately. The chair must reconvene the meeting at the stated time or after the agreed duration. After a recess, the meeting carries on from the point at which the recess began.

4. Adjourn

The motion to adjourn is used to close a meeting and has been discussed earlier in this book. It is usually a simple matter of formality; however, members need not wait until all business is concluded to make a motion to adjourn. Provided it is not qualified in any way, this motion must be treated as a privileged motion.

The meeting is not actually over until the chair makes the declaration that "The meeting stands adjourned." This last step is another part of maintaining control of the meeting at all of its stages.

5. Fix the time to which to adjourn

It is not uncommon to discover that the time allocated for a meeting is insufficient to deal with all the business on the agenda. This is often handled by adding the leftover items to the next meeting under the unfinished business section.

Sometimes, however, it is desirable, or even necessary, to complete all items from the current meeting before the next regular meeting of the organization. In this case a motion to fix the time to which to adjourn is employed. It is used to set the time when this adjourned meeting will reconvene. Such a meeting must take place before the next regularly scheduled meeting. This kind of adjourned meeting is not a new session, merely a continuation of the previous one, and business resumes at the point where it was interrupted.

The motion must specify the exact time and place:

> *I move that when we adjourn, we adjourn to meet on Wednesday night at 6:30 p.m. in this meeting room.*

c. INCIDENTAL MOTIONS

This class of motion deals mostly with procedural matters. These motions arise out of the debate on pending questions, but they do not relate to that business directly. Thus, they are referred to as incidental. These kinds of motions are not ranked in any way; they are dealt with as they arise. The chair must use common sense in disposing of these kinds of motions.

Three incidental motions that deal with the rules of order are touched on here. For information on how to deal with the many other motions of this type, you should consult *Robert's Rules of Order (Newly Revised)*.

1. Point of order

When the rules of debate and procedure have been violated, it is the duty of the chair to enforce the proper rule. If the chair fails to do so, any individual member may immediately rise on a point of order. An example of a breach of order is when the chair allows discussion on a motion to take place without that motion being seconded.

The point of order may interrupt a speaker, and the form is as follows:

Mr. President, I rise on a point of order.

A point of order must be raised as soon as the breach occurs.

The chair must rule on the member's point before debate can continue. If no violation has taken place, then the chair will often say, "Your point is not well taken," and explain the reason. If the chair agrees that a rule has been broken, the response is "Your point is well taken," and an explanation and remedy is given.

Decisions on points of order should be made as quickly as possible. Even inexperienced presiding officers will be able to decide on most points if they have studied even a simple primer such as this book. Sometimes the issue is rather complicated and outside the expertise of the chair. In this case, it is best for the chair to declare a short recess for the purpose of consulting a rule book.

NEVER try to fake it. It is ALWAYS better to admit ignorance and search for the right answer. There is no shame in saying you do not know the proper ruling. Taking the trouble to be correct will be appreciated by your membership; it shows that you put proper conduct ahead of your own ego.

2. Appeal the decision of the chair

The ruling of the chair can be appealed. The purpose of an appeal is to reverse the decision made by the chair. It takes two people to initiate the appeal: one to make the motion, another to second it. To be valid, an appeal of the chair's ruling must be made immediately after the ruling. The form is as follows:

Member #1: *Mr. Chairman, I appeal the decision of the chair.*

Member #2: *Mr. Chairman, I second the motion.*

Chair: *The decision of the chair has been appealed. Shall the decision of the chair stand?*

If the chair's question is passed, the chair says "The decision of the chair stands." If defeated, the chair says "The decision of the chair is reversed."

3. Suspend the rules

A motion to suspend the rules is used when an assembly wishes to do something that is against its regular rules of procedure (but NOT in conflict with the basic constitution or bylaws of the organization). The reason for having to suspend the rules is usually to allow a speaker to be heard at a particular time or to deal with a piece of business out of order. Examples are —

I move that the rules be suspended for the purpose of hearing our guest speaker.

I move that the rules be suspended because Ms. X has to leave by 3 p.m., and her information is vital to consideration of Item #2 under New Business.

d. REVIEW OF THE RANKINGS

There are three types of motions in addition to the common main motion: subsidiary motions, privileged motions, and incidental motions. The seven subsidiary motions and the five privileged motions have a pre-determined priority. Incidental motions are not ranked.

Any privileged motion outranks a subsidiary or a main motion. Taken as a group, all motions can be ranked as follows (from lowest priority to the highest):

(a) Main motion

(b) Subsidiary motions

    (1) Postpone indefinitely

    (2) Amend

    (3) Commit or refer

    (4) Postpone definitely (to a certain time)

    (5) Limit or extend debate

    (6) Previous question

    (7) Lay on the table

(c) Privileged motions

    (1) Call for the orders of the day

    (2) Raise a question of privilege

    (3) Take a recess

    (4) Adjourn

    (5) Fix the time to which to adjourn

TABLE #1
SUMMARY OF THE RULES OF MOTIONS

MAIN MOTION

Can it interrupt a speaker?	NO
Does it require a seconder?	YES
Is it debatable?	YES
Is it amendable?	YES
What vote is required to pass?	MAJORITY

SUBSIDIARY MOTIONS

Postpone indefinitely

Can it interrupt a speaker?	NO
Does it require a seconder?	YES
Is it debatable?	YES
Is it amendable?	NO
What vote is required to pass?	MAJORITY

Amend

Can it interrupt a speaker?	NO
Does it require a seconder?	YES
Is it debatable?	YES
Is it amendable?	YES
What vote is required to pass?	MAJORITY

Commit or refer

Can it interrupt a speaker?	NO
Does it require a seconder?	YES
Is it debatable?	YES
Is it amendable?	YES
What vote is required to pass?	MAJORITY

Postpone definitely

Can it interrupt a speaker?	NO
Does it require a seconder?	YES
Is it debatable?	YES
Is it amendable?	YES
What vote is required to pass?	MAJORITY

TABLE #1 — Continued

Limit or extend debate

Can it interrupt a speaker?	NO
Does it require a seconder?	YES
Is it debatable?	NO
Is it amendable?	YES
What vote is required to pass?	TWO-THIRDS

Previous question

Can it interrupt a speaker?	NO
Does it require a seconder?	YES
Is it debatable?	NO
Is it amendable?	NO
What vote is required to pass?	TWO-THIRDS

Lay on the table

Can it interrupt a speaker?	NO
Does it require a seconder?	YES
Is it debatable?	NO
Is it amendable?	NO
What vote is required to pass?	MAJORITY

PRIVILEGED MOTIONS

Call for the orders of the day

Can it interrupt a speaker?	YES
Does it require a seconder?	NO
Is it debatable?	NO
Is it amendable?	NO
What vote is required to pass?	NONE*

Question of privilege

Can it interrupt a speaker?	YES
Does it require a seconder?	NO
Is it debatable?	NO
Is it amendable?	NO
What vote is required to pass?	NONE*

TABLE #1 — Continued

Take a recess

Can it interrupt a speaker?	NO
Does it require a seconder?	YES
Is it debatable?	NO
Is it amendable?	YES
What vote is required to pass?	MAJORITY

Adjourn

Can it interrupt a speaker?	NO
Does it require a seconder?	YES
Is it debatable?	NO
Is it amendable?	NO
What vote is required to pass?	MAJORITY

Fix the time to which to adjourn

Can it interrupt a speaker?	NO
Does it require a seconder?	YES
Is it debatable?	NO
Is it amendable?	YES
What vote is required to pass?	MAJORITY

INCIDENTAL MOTIONS

Suspend the rules

Can it interrupt a speaker?	NO
Does it require a seconder?	YES
Is it debatable?	NO
Is it amendable?	NO
What vote is required to pass?	TWO-THIRDS

Appeal the decision of the chair

Can it interrupt a speaker?	YES
Does it require a seconder?	YES
Is it debatable?	NO
Is it amendable?	NO
What vote is required to pass?	MAJORITY OR TIE

TABLE #1 — Continued

Point of order

Can it interrupt a speaker?	YES
Does it require a seconder?	NO
Is it debatable?	NO
Is it amendable?	NO
What vote is required to pass?	NONE*

* Decided by the chair

5
COMMITTEES AND REPORTS

In most organizations, a great deal of the work is accomplished by committees. There are some basic advantages to deliberations by committees rather than by larger assemblies: committee meetings are smaller, less formal, and often made up of people specially selected for their expertise and/or enthusiasm.

There are many different kinds of committees, each serving a specific function. The nature of the committee will determine things such as the frequency of meeting, the topics referred to it, and the kind of reports required.

In this chapter, there is a short discussion of the main types of committees, how their meetings should be conducted, and how to deal with their reports.

a. TYPES OF COMMITTEES

1. Executive committee

An executive committee usually consists of the officers of the organization (i.e., president, vice president, secretary, treasurer, etc.). Individually and as a group, this committee acts on behalf of the organization between its regular meetings. The specific duties of the officers and the authority for them to act as an executive committee should be detailed in the bylaws of your organization.

2. Standing committee

A standing committee is a permanent committee, and it exists to deal with a regular issue, department, or activity. As with the officers and executive committee, the name, composition, selection, and scope of duties of any standing committee should be specified in the bylaws.

It is common for a standing committee to have the power to act independently within its sphere of responsibility without instruction from the whole assembly. For example, your group might create a permanent standing committee to handle the annual banquet. It would be appropriate for that committee to make all of the arrangements without having to get approval for every detail.

Aside from any "statutory" duties assigned to it by the organization's constitution, a standing committee may handle matters referred to it by specific motion of the whole organization.

3. Special or select committee

This kind of committee is created by the organization for one specific task, and it ceases to exist when that task is completed and its final report is presented. Another common name for this type of committee is an ad hoc committee. Any committee not specified in the organization's bylaws or constitution as a standing committee must, therefore, be constituted as a special or select committee.

The motion creating a committee for a special purpose must be specific on several points:

- The task or subject to be referred
- The composition of the committee
- The time allowed to report
- Whether the committee is empowered to take any action, or just report recommendations to the group

Typical examples of a motion to create a select or special committee are as follows:

I move that a committee be struck to nominate a slate of candidates for the executive positions. Said committee will consist of Member X, Member Y, and Member Z and will report back to this assembly in two weeks' time.

I move that a committee be set up to handle the repairs to our kitchen. The committee will be made up of three members to be chosen by the treasurer, and it will have the power to get estimates for the work and proceed with any work under $500. Expenditures over $500 will have to be approved by a regular meeting.

4. Committee of the whole

This is a rare type of committee for most organizations to employ, but it can be useful. It is created by a motion that "This assembly do resolve itself into committee of the whole for the purpose of dealing with (a specific motion or item of business)." If such a motion is passed, the whole assembly immediately becomes a committee of the whole.

The reason for resorting to this form of committee is to allow a complicated or contentious matter to be dealt with in the more informal atmosphere of a committee (see section **b. RULES AND DECORUM IN COMMITTEE** below).

In committee, the presiding officer of the main assembly meeting usually relinquishes the chair to the next most senior executive officer, usually the vice president.

b. RULES AND DECORUM IN COMMITTEE

1. The chair

The choice of a person to preside at the committee meetings is sometimes troublesome. The best way of avoiding any problems is to have the matter settled when the members are selected to the committee. With a standing committee, the chair could be assigned to the first person elected. With select or special committees, the motion to set it up should state who will act as chair.

In committee, the chair is permitted to engage in active debate and offer opinions on the matters at hand. The chair of a committee can vote on all motions.

It is the duty of the chair of the committee to call all meetings. The chair is ultimately responsible for ensuring that the committee's mandate is carried out within any time limitations imposed on it by assembly.

In most cases, the chair of the committee keeps a written record of what is decided during the meeting. If it seems desirable and necessary, a secretary can be designated. The presiding officer prepares the final committee report for presentation to the main body of the organization.

2. Rules of procedure

In general, committee meetings are far less formal than regular meetings of the entire organization. The key features of this informality are the following:

- Members do not need to be recognized to obtain the floor to speak or make a motion.
- There is no limitation on debate. Members may speak as long as they like as often as they like.
- Motions do not need to be seconded.
- There does not have to be a formal motion on the floor for the chair to call for a vote on a particular issue.

In keeping with this notion of allowing unlimited debate, the motions "to limit debate" and "the previous question" are not used in committee.

Without the buttress of all the formal rules of procedure, the presiding officer of a committee can often be faced with the need for more subtle means of control — for control must still be maintained in a committee meeting. Notwithstanding the tradition of unlimited debate in committee, the chair must tactfully ensure that one member does not monopolize the discussion. Nor should repetitive and irrelevant debate be permitted.

Unless otherwise specified in the bylaws, the quorum of any committee is a majority of its designated members.

c. REPORTS OF COMMITTEES

Committees operate under instructions from the whole organization. Therefore, they are responsible to the organization and must report on their activities. A majority of the members of the committee must approve the report before it can be presented to the main assembly.

1. Form of reports

On rare occasions, a brief verbal report by the committee chair is appropriate. However, in most cases, a written report is prepared by the chair and, if approved by the majority of the committee, submitted during a regular meeting of the organization. Because the report represents the decisions and/or recommendations of the majority of the committee, not just the presiding officer who wrote it, the report must be written in the third person (e.g., "The committee presents its findings in this report. They...").

2. Content of reports

The content and level of detail of a committee report will naturally vary depending on the function of the committee and the matter(s) referred to in it. Committee reports should include the following basic information:

- A summary of the matter referred to it, or a summary of its permanent mandate

- A list of the number of times the committee met since it was created (for select or special committees), or how often it has met since its last report (for standing committees)

- A summary of how the committee proceeded with its task
- A summary of the actions taken or information gathered
- Any recommendations approved by the committee (with any accompanying resolutions for the main assembly)

Samples #2 and #3 show two different styles of committee reports. Sample #2, a special committee report, is a recommendation to the main assembly. It requires further action by that assembly. Since this committee is a "Special Committee," it ceases to exist once it makes its report. Sample #3 is a permanent committee report and is simply for the information of the main assembly. This committee has the power to make changes in policy (within its terms of reference) and to expend funds from its own account. It does not require any action by the meeting.

3. Presentation and consideration of reports

Reports from committees are usually included under routine business on the agenda. Reports should be distributed in written form; in addition, they can be read aloud — either by the secretary or the presiding officer of the committee.

If the report is merely a statement of actions taken by the committee, and those actions are in accord with its terms of reference, the report is simply filed. If a matter referred to the committee called for recommendations, those recommendations should be included in the report as resolutions or notice that motions will be forthcoming. If the recommendations are put forward as main motions, this is usually done by the chair of the committee.

Sometimes a motion, rather than a task, is referred to a committee. Once the committee has made its report, that motion automatically comes back to the assembly (usually under unfinished business). The motion comes before the meeting in its original form regardless of what the committee recommends about disposition of the motion. If the committee recommends changes to the motion, they may be moved in the usual way as amendments.

4. Minority reports

Committee members who disagree with the report presented by the chair of the committee can submit a report of the views of the minority. To be legitimate, a minority report must deal with matters of opinion and interpretation only. Typically, a minority report is a set of recommendations meant to be alternatives to the official committee report.

SAMPLE #2
SPECIAL COMMITTEE REPORT

The chair of the Special Committee on Examination Writing submits the following report on the Committee's activities:

The committee was charged with investigating the implications of changing from ink to pencil as the required medium for examinations. We were asked to prepare recommendations for presentation at this meeting (biannual executive meeting) and were given the authority to expend funds up to a total of $950.

The committee met three times (December 6, January 17, and May 5) to discuss the issue. After the initial meeting, it was clear that the members lacked sufficient expertise to make a decision without further information. The second meeting was spent deciding to engage three consultants who were recognized authorities in document preparation, presentation, and preservation. Each consultant was asked to submit a written report by February 28. The cost for each was $200.

All three reports were received by the chair before the deadline date. These reports were circulated to the members of the committee, and when we met for the third time, it was determined that we had ample background information to come to a decision.

Based on our own subjective experience, which is reinforced by all of the experts we consulted, your committee recommends that no change be made to the present system of "ink only" examination writing.

The chair of the Standing Committee on Examination Writing submits the following report on the Committee's activities:

The committee met three times (December 6, January 17, and May 5) since its last report. As part of its ongoing investigation of examination procedures, the committee has instituted a policy change regarding the use of pencils during examinations.

To provide sufficient detail for an informed decision, the committee decided to engage three consultants who were recognized authorities in document preparation, presentation, and preservation. Each consultant was asked to submit a written report by February 28. The cost for each was $200. All three reports were received by the chair before the deadline. These reports were circulated to the members of the committee, and when we met for the third time, it was determined that we had ample background information to come to a decision.

Based on our own subjective experience, which is reinforced by all of the experts we consulted, your committee decided to allow the use of both pens and pencils during written examinations. The issue of the acceptability of colored pencils is still under consideration.

6
ELECTIONS

All organizations hold elections of some sort at some time. Usually these elections are for executive offices, regular directors, or delegates to conventions. This process is greatly simplified if the organization has made detailed provisions in its bylaws. The details required include positions to be filled, duties of those elected, qualifications to hold office, how nominations are to be made, and how voting is to take place.

If your bylaws do not have this information, AMEND THEM SOON. Because of the very personal nature of the kind of decision being made, few things can be as divisive as club or society elections. Try to ensure that the actual process of the election does not become a problem. Running a smooth election is an excellent measure of the quality of a presiding officer.

Here are some simple, commonsense guidelines to consider if your bylaws are not adequate.

In the case of filling single offices, it is easiest to deal with one position at a time (i.e., go through the nomination and voting steps for president, then vice president, and so on).

a. NOMINATIONS

1. By committee

In large organizations, or those that do not meet very often, it is common to establish a slate of nominees for each office by referring the matter to a nominations committee. Such a committee should itself be elected. If it is not a standing committee provided for in the constitution, then the motion that creates it should be very specific about its mandate:

> *I move that a special nominations committee be established, and that said committee be comprised of seven people elected at this meeting. The nominations committee is to establish a list of no less than one nominee for each executive office and present its report at the annual general meeting.*

Unfortunately, the use of such a committee is often misunderstood and gives rise to resentment and the feeling that election to office is "fixed" and unfair. The real purpose of a nominating committee is to make sure that people separated by large distances have an opportunity to be nominated or have input into the nomination process. It allows the process of selection to be carried out over a longer period of time than just the day of the meeting, which is beneficial in an organization where members are not well known to each other.

Once the report of the nomination committee is received, the chair declares the person(s) in the report to be duly nominated. At that point, the chair asks if there are any nominations from the floor. In the interests of fairness, an organization should never adopt a system that precludes nominations from the floor. Regardless of the quality of the work of a nominations committee, the organization as a whole must feel that it is in control of its leadership selection.

2.   From the floor

If there has been a report submitted by a nominations committee, the chair should state something like —

> *Ms. X has been duly nominated for the position of president.*

Then nominations can be made by anyone at the meeting. The chair should inform the meeting when it is time to make nominations by asking —

> *Are there any nominations from the floor for the position of president?*

If there is no nominating committee, then the election process begins with the chair declaring—

> *The floor is now open for nominations for the position of president.*

To prevent chaos, the chair should insist that members be properly recognized before they can make a nomination. Members nominate someone with the statement —

> *Mr. Chairman, I nominate Mr. Z for the position of president.*

Since no one can be forced to serve in office, the chair should ask the member if he or she wishes to be nominated. The standard forms for this step are the following:

> *Does Mr. Z consent to the nomination?*

> *Will Mr. Z allow his name to stand?*

If the member refuses nomination, that ends the matter. If he or she accepts the nomination, the chair says —

> *Mr. Z is duly nominated. Are there any further nominations?*

3. Closing nominations

When no further nominations are forthcoming, the chair should say the following:

Are there any further nominations for the office of president? Hearing none, the chair declares nominations closed.

If only one person is nominated for a particular office, then that person is declared elected by acclamation, and the chair should say the following:

There being no other nominations for the position of president, the chair declares Mr. Z elected by acclamation.

b. VOTING

Many other books discuss a variety of ways to conduct the vote during elections. But the simplest and most effective is the secret ballot. Unless your organization's bylaws stipulate an alternative method, or there is some other compelling reason, the secret ballot should always be used for voting.

1. Counters or tellers

Before the vote begins, the presiding officer appoints at least three people to act as tellers. Their duties are to collect, count, and tabulate the ballots.

Obviously, no one appointed a teller should be a candidate for that particular office.

2. Balloting

Sometimes the ballots can be prepared in advance of the voting, but this is rare. Plenty of printed blank ballots should be available for the voting. If this is not possible, plain blank paper is always acceptable.

Once blank ballots have been distributed, the chair should remind the members what position is being filled and who the candidates are. Try to have a blackboard, or something similar, so that the names can be displayed for all to see.

3. Spoiled ballots

Before balloting begins, the chair must explain how the ballots are to be marked. What constitutes a valid vote and what will result in a spoiled ballot must be absolutely clear to every member. The chair must never assume everyone knows what is going on; everything should be explained in detail.

For example, if there are four nominees for president, the chair should instruct the members as follows:

> *There is only one person to be elected, so vote for ONE PERSON ONLY. If the ballot is completed or marked in any way that makes it appear that more than one person has been voted for, the tellers are instructed to regard that as a spoiled ballot and it will not be counted.*

If there are four vacancies on the board of directors, and there are seven nominees, the chair should explain to the voters the following:

> *There are four directors to be elected. You can vote for one, two, three, or four people. If you vote for more than four, you will spoil your ballot. You may vote for less than four if you wish.*

4. Counting the ballots

The tellers collect the ballots, making certain that they receive only one from each member. Before counting begins, the chair should ask if everyone has submitted their ballots to a teller.

The tellers usually leave the room to count the ballots. The first thing the tellers do is ensure that there are not more ballots than members present. They then count the votes and prepare a report for the chair. This report should include —

- Total votes cast
- Total votes for each candidate

- Number of spoiled or invalid ballots

5. Announcing the results

The tellers do not determine a result or declare that anyone is elected. The chair must do that after reading the tellers' report. It is good form for the chair to read the entire report. For example —

> *There were 45 votes cast, 4 of which were spoiled ballots. The 41 valid ballots were cast as follows:*
>
> *Mr. X: 5*
>
> *Ms. Y: 7*
>
> *Mr. W: 12*
>
> *Mrs. F: 17*
>
> *Mrs. F is declared ELECTED.*

6. Plurality or majority

In most elections, it is usually a matter of "whoever gets the most votes wins." This is known as the plurality system or "first past the post." A person does not have to receive a majority of the votes: he or she must simply have more than anyone else. Thus, Mrs. F is elected with only 41.5% of the valid votes cast.

If an organization's bylaws require a majority for election, and there are more than two candidates, there is potential for complications. If a majority is called for in the bylaws, there should also be instructions for conducting further votes. Obviously Mrs. F has not received a majority (defined as 50% plus 1). What is done next?

If there is no stipulation in the constitution, then traditional practice indicates that the person with the lowest vote total is deleted from the list of candidates. Thus, Mr. X is dropped, and the vote is held again. If there is still no majority winner, then the third place finisher is dropped and a third ballot is held between the two remaining nominees.

7. Disposal of ballots

The ballots should be kept for a predetermined length of time (e.g., one month or until the next meeting) in case there is any dispute of the results. They should be sealed after the results are announced, and kept by the secretary. After the stipulated time, the ballots should be destroyed.

It is common for someone at the meeting to make a motion that the ballots be destroyed immediately. This is not a good practice and should be avoided. The chair should take time to explain the necessity of retaining the ballots intact for awhile.

7

HELP:
GOING TO A HIGHER AUTHORITY

As stated at the outset, this book is meant as a simplified introduction to the rules and procedures that govern formal meetings. It is not intended to be a definitive resource. The information presented here should prepare you for just about any situation, but it does not cover everything. If you spend enough time as the chair, especially if you belong to several different types of organizations, situations will arise that cannot be dealt with by the basics in this book. At that point, you will have to refer to a "higher authority." This authority is most often a comprehensive manual of parliamentary procedure, but it can be a specially trained person called a parliamentarian.

a. PARLIAMENTARY AUTHORITY

1. What is it?

The parliamentary authority is the manual of parliamentary law that your organization has adopted as its reference source for all issues of rules and procedure. It is the bible for all decisions related to procedure.

Every organization should specify a parliamentary authority in its bylaws. If this concept is new to you, then yours is probably one of the many groups that have neglected this item in its constitution. It is understandable that the matter of what rule book to use at meetings may not seem terribly significant when creating the constitution for an organization. Nonetheless, it is important, and a little attention paid to selecting a parliamentary authority can save time and trouble later on. If your bylaws do not contain a reference to a parliamentary authority, you should amend them to include one.

Once a parliamentary authority is established for your organization, no other rules of order apply. Thus, in any disputes over procedure or interpretation of rules the existence of contradictory evidence in another book is irrelevant.

2. When to use it

Although a parliamentary authority can be very significant, it must be admitted that you will hardly ever have to refer to it. But when you do, you will be very glad it exists. It can save a lot of time that might be wasted over procedural wrangling.

There are three basic situations that result in the chair having to seek the advice of the written parliamentary authority:

(a) When the chair is unsure of how to proceed in a routine matter (This situation will not arise very frequently as the chair gains experience and expertise.)

(b) When the chair is faced with a totally new situation, especially one not covered in an introductory manual such as this

(c) When the ruling of the chair is challenged or appealed

As has been stated earlier, never hesitate to check an authority if you are unsure of a rule or its applicability. Getting it right is always more important than the chair's ego.

3. Choosing a parliamentary authority

There are many choices available to your organization, and some serious thought should go into the selection of your parliamentary authority. As always, the primary factor should be common sense. A small local club is hardly likely to require the resources of the 594 pages of *Robert's Rules of Order (Newly Revised)*. In fact, such a manual will probably be so unwieldy as to be utterly useless. A national association of professionals, with an annual general meeting that may attract hundreds of participants, could benefit from having this kind of backup however.

As a guide to the selection of a parliamentary authority, Appendix 2 provides some descriptive details about a few of the possible manuals.

4. How to include it in your bylaws

Ideally, adoption of a parliamentary authority should be included in your bylaws or constitution in the development stage. If this did not happen, the oversight can be rectified by an amendment. (The amendment process will differ among organizations.)

The provision can be as simple as the following:

> *The rules contained in Gumby's Rules of Order (34th edition) shall govern the meetings of this society insofar as they are applicable and do not conflict with the present or future bylaws of the society.*

If you wish to devise a simplified set of rules specifically suited to your organization (see chapter 8 for guidelines on how to do this), this should be noted in your bylaws along with reference to another parliamentary authority as a contingency:

> *The rules contained in the document entitled Rules of Order for Freelance Association of Regulatory Technicians (1881) shall govern the meetings of this society insofar as they are applicable and do not conflict with the present or future bylaws of the society. Matters not provided for in the aforementioned document shall be dealt with*

according to the procedures set out in Gumby's
Rules of Order (34th edition).

Robert's Rules of Order (Newly Revised) notes that some organizations, such as unions, registered non-profit societies, and professional associations, are also governed by municipal, state, provincial, and/or national laws. It may be prudent to recognize this in the bylaw provision for a parliamentary authority:

> *The rules contained in Gumby's Rules of Order (34th edition) shall govern the meetings of this society insofar as they are applicable and do not conflict with the present or future bylaws of the society, or any statutes applicable to the society.*

b. PROFESSIONAL PARLIAMENTARIAN

1. What is it?

A parliamentarian is a professional expert in rules of order. A professional parliamentarian serves as a consultant and advisor to the presiding officer and, in some cases, to the membership in general. He or she is appointed by the chair or president and is usually paid by the organization.

Anyone can set up as a consultant, but genuine professional parliamentarians are those who are certified by, or registered with, one of the international parliamentary associations (see below).

The parliamentarian's role is purely advisory. The chair should consult with the parliamentarian before the meeting in order to avoid interruptions later on. The chair may ask for advice, but the parliamentarian NEVER makes rulings — that remains the prerogative of the chair. A parliamentarian is also bound to acknowledge the rules of order and parliamentary authority adopted by the organization.

2. When to use one

Most routine meetings do not require the services of a parliamentarian, but a parliamentarian can be a useful assistant to the chair during large and especially important meetings or when the business to be conducted is likely to become complicated and/or contentious.

3. Where to find one

If you are convinced that you require the services of a professional parliamentarian, make certain you get one that is reliable. The best way to do this is to write to a parliamentary association. The American Institute of Parliamentarians (A.I.P.) and the National Association of Parliamentarians (N.A.P.) maintain lists of qualified people and will be happy to send you the names of parliamentarians available in your area.

Addresses for both the A.I.P. and N.A.P. are listed in Appendix 2.

8
DO IT YOURSELF: HOW TO WRITE RULES FOR YOUR OWN GROUP

What should be obvious from the tone and presentation of material in this book is that "parliamentary procedure" can be flexible, and its primary purpose is to *serve* your organization — not dominate it.

Within the natural constraints of common sense and the general principles confirmed through years of satisfactory application, the essential rules of order can be adapted to meet the needs of just about any organization. Given this premise, it is perfectly logical and acceptable for many groups to decide to construct a basic set of rules tailored to their customs and requirements.

There are four kinds of rules that can be devised to govern an organization:

(a) constitution,

(b) bylaws,

(c) standing rules, and

(d) rules of order.

The first two of these are self-explanatory and outside the scope of this book. (Ray Keesey's book, *Barnes & Noble Book of Modern Parliamentary Procedure,* has a helpful section on this subject. See Appendix 2.)

Standing rules deal with details such as the standard date, time and place of meetings, the conduct of guests, etc.

Rules of order are entirely separate and are concerned exclusively with procedural matters.

a. GUIDELINES FOR DEVELOPING YOUR OWN RULES

If you wish to develop a set of rules of order specifically for use by your organization, here are a few guidelines to follow:

(a) This document does not replace any part of the constitution or bylaws; it becomes an adjunct to them.

(b) Keep it short and simple. The whole point of this exercise is to create a document that will make parliamentary procedure more accessible to your membership. Ideally, your specially designed rules of order should not exceed two to three pages.

(c) Your "customized" rules of order should include those rules commonly encountered in the course of a typical meeting as well as those that differ from the recommendations in your parliamentary authority.

(d) Make sure you have adopted a credible parliamentary authority and formally included it in your bylaws or constitution (see chapter 7). It is a good idea to refer to this authority in your rules of order, but it must first appear in the bylaws. This is important because it is quite simple to suspend the basic rules of order for special purposes, but you do not want to suspend all parliamentary authority, which is what would happen if the power of the parliamentary authority is mentioned only in the rules of order.

(e) Before they are passed by your group, take the time and trouble to have your proposed rules checked by someone who is familiar with parliamentary procedure. Even if there is a small consulting fee charged for this service, it is worth it. See chapter 7 for an example of the motion used to approve a set of rules specific to your organization.

b. COMPONENTS OF YOUR RULES OF ORDER

The following are just a few of the standard items that can be included in a "do-it-yourself" set of rules. The italicized sample rules are only suggestions. Exactly how many rules you decide to include, and the precise wording of those rules, is up to you. As long as you do not deviate too much from accepted parliamentary practice and employ even a modicum of common sense, you should be able to write something that will be genuinely useful and authoritative for your organization.

1. Title

Give a title to your rules of order that includes the name of the organization and the year the rules were approved (and updated or revised if applicable). For example —

> *Rules of Order for the Freelance Association of Scintillating Syncopators (August, 1980; revised December, 1988).*

2. Parliamentary authority

Include a reference to your adopted parliamentary authority (see section **a.** above). The following shows the proper form for doing this:

> *Matters not provided for in these rules shall be dealt with according to the procedures set out in Gumby's Rules of Order (34th edition).*

3. Quorum

Consider the issue of quorum carefully (see chapter 1). Make certain that the number you set for quorum is reasonable for your organization. As with the parliamentary authority, the quorum should first be established in the bylaws. An appropriate form for statement in the rules of order is as follows:

> *The minimum number of members that must be present at any meeting for the proper conduct of business must be 15 current members in good standing.*

4. Order of business

If you wish to formalize the order of proceedings at your meetings, you can do that by listing the proposed order.

(a) Call to order

(b) Routine business

    (i) Approval of agenda

    (ii) Approval of minutes

    (iii) Communications

    (iv) Reports

(c) Business arising from the minutes

(d) New business

(e) Adjournment

5. Length and number of speeches

As with the matter of quorum, consider this matter carefully. Your decision on the length and number of speeches allowed should reflect what is reasonable for your particular situation. Examples of rules dealing with these issues are —

> *Except for the mover of a main motion, no member shall speak more than once to a main motion. The mover of a main motion may be allowed to speak a second time and in doing so shall close debate on the motion.*

Individual speeches shall not exceed ten (10) minutes in length. In committee, no such limit shall apply.

6. Methods of voting

If you wish to have the method of voting specified, be very clear about what is required.

All voting shall initially be by voice. If unable to declare an outcome on this basis, the chair may call for a show of hands. If three or more members present indicate disagreement with the chair's declaration of the voice vote, another vote shall be conducted by a show of hands.

APPENDIX 1
CHART OF COMMON MOTIONS
(Tear out for reference)

MOTION	RULES GOVERNING MOTIONS				
	Interrupt speaker	Seconder required	Debatable	Amendable	Vote required to pass
PRIVILEGED MOTIONS					
Fix time to which to adjourn	NO	YES	NO	YES	Majority
Adjourn	NO	YES	NO	NO	Majority
Take a recess	NO	YES	NO	YES	Majority
Question of privilege	YES	NO	NO	NO	None*
Call for the orders of the day	YES	NO	NO	NO	None*
SUBSIDIARY MOTIONS					
Lay on the table	NO	YES	NO	NO	Majority
Previous question	NO	YES	NO	NO	Two-thirds
Limit or extend debate	NO	YES	NO	YES	Two-thirds
Postpone definitely	NO	YES	YES	YES	Majority
Commit or refer	NO	YES	YES	YES	Majority
Amend	NO	YES	YES	YES	Majority
Postpone indefinitely	NO	YES	YES	NO	Majority
MAIN MOTIONS	NO	YES	YES	YES	Majority
INCIDENTAL MOTIONS					
Point of order	YES	NO	NO	NO	None*
Appeal the decision of the chair	YES	YES	NO	NO	Majority or a tie
Suspend the rules	NO	YES	NO	NO	Two-thirds

*Decided by the chair

APPENDIX 2
OTHER SOURCES

a. BOOKS

The books listed here are just a small sampling of those available on the subject of parliamentary procedure and rules of order. A complete bibliography would take several pages and probably result in more confusion than clarification. Any of these are suitable as a parliamentary authority depending on the needs of your organization.

The two editions of *Robert's Rules of Order* and the new edition of Alice Sturgis's book are by far the most comprehensive and may be more than is required for most groups. *Robert's* is very traditional, while the main thrust of Sturgis is to attempt some modernization of process and terminology. If you decide to use an exhaustive source, two other books that merit attention are *Demeter's Manual of Parliamentary Law and Procedure* by George Demeter and *Riddick's Rules of Procedure* by Floyd Riddick, former parliamentarian of the U.S. Senate.

Keesey and Farwell go even further in trying to simplify and modernize. Either of those books would be a good choice if you prefer something less imposing.

Bourinot, Sir John George. *Bourinot's Rules of Order.* (ed. Geoffrey H. Stanford). Toronto: McClelland and Stewart, 1977. 112 pages.

Farwell, H.G. *The Majority Rules: A Manual of Procedure for MOST Groups.* Pueblo, Colorado: High Publishers, 1988. 112 pages.

Jones, O. Garfield. *Parliamentary Procedure at a Glance.* New York: Hawthorn Books, 1971. 68 pages.

Keesey, Ray E. *Barnes & Noble Book of Modern Parliamentary Procedure.* New York: Barnes & Noble Books/Harper and Row, 1974. 176 pages.

Robert, Henry M. *Robert's Rules of Order* (ed. Rachel Vixman). New York: Jove Books/Berkeley Publishing Group, 1986. 204 pages.

Robert, Henry M. *Robert's Rules of Order (Newly Revised)* (ed. Sarah Corbin Robert). Glenview, Illinois: Scott, Foresman and Company, 1970. 594 pages.

Ryan, Stanley M. *Parliamentary Procedure: Essential Principles.* Cranbury, N.J.: Cornwall Books, 1985. 227 pages.

Sturgis, Alice. *Standard Code of Parliamentary Procedure (3rd edition — New and Revised).* New York: McGraw-Hill, 1988. 275 pages.

b. PARLIAMENTARY ORGANIZATIONS

The American Institute of Parliamentarians offers a program of education, training, and examination leading to the designations of Certified Parliamentarian and Certified Professional Parliamentarian. For more information, write to —

American Institute of Parliamentarians
P.O. Box 12452
Fort Wayne, Indiana 46863

The National Association of Parliamentarians has a similar system of professional development and certification. Their designations are Registered Parliamentarian and Professional Registered Parliamentarian.

National Association of Parliamentarians
6601 Winchester Avenue, Suite 260
Kansas City, Missouri 64133-4600

ANOTHER TITLE IN THE
SELF-COUNSEL SERIES

THE MINUTE TAKER'S HANDBOOK
Taking Minutes at Any Meeting With Confidence
by Jane Watson

The minute taker of today's meeting assumes a great responsibility. He or she is the chronicler of the group, the one who harnesses the whirlwind of information, synthesizes it into a clear, understandable form, and ultimately dispenses a formal record of the proceedings.

This practical book is designed to help minute takers become more confident in their recording skills. It provides techniques and examples to enable note takers to produce concise, accurate minutes in a timely manner. It also defines the role of the minute taker, covering everying from setting objectives to producing a summary, coordinating audio-visual equipment to deciding on a seating plan. The book not only helps minute takers polish organizational effectiveness, it details skills to help maximize the efficiency of the meeting for all those involved. $8.95

ORDERING INFORMATION

All prices are subject to change without notice. Books are available in book, department, and stationery stores. If you cannot buy the book through a store, please use this order form. (Please print)

IN CANADA

Please send your order to the nearest location:
Self-Counsel Press, 1481 Charlotte Road,
North Vancouver, B. C. V7J 1H1
Self-Counsel Press, 8-2283 Argentia Road,
Mississauga, Ontario L5N 5Z2
Add 7% GST to the cost of the books.
Add $2.68 ($2.50 for postage & handling, $.18 GST)

IN THE U.S.A.

Please send your order to:
Self-Counsel Press Inc., 1704 N. State Street,
Bellingham, WA 98225
Add $2.50 for postage and handling.
WA residents please add 7.8% sales tax.

Name_____

Address_____

_____

Charge to:
❏Visa   ❏ MasterCard

Account Number_____

Validation Date _____

Expiry Date_____

Signature_____

❏**Check here for a free catalogue.**

Yes, please send me:
_____copies of **The Minute Taker's Handbook,** $8.95
_____copies of **Chairing a Meeting,** $7.95